Nineteen Gardens

Magdalena Miecznicka

T0179852

methuen | drama

LONDON • NEW YORK • OXFORD • NEW DELHI • SYDNEY

METHUEN DRAMA
Bloomsbury Publishing Plc
50 Bedford Square, London, WC1B 3DP, UK
1385 Broadway, New York, NY 10018, USA
29 Earlsfort Terrace, Dublin 2, Ireland

BLOOMSBURY, METHUEN DRAMA and the Methuen
Drama logo are trademarks of Bloomsbury Publishing Plc

First published in Great Britain 2023

Cover images: Adam Kring (green door), Jon Tyson
(brown door), and Donald Giannatti (vine) on Unsplash

A catalogue record for this book is available from the British Library.

A catalog record for this book is available from the Library of Congress.

ISBN: PB: 978-1-3504-5522-1
ePDF: 978-1-3504-5523-8
eBook: 978-1-3504-5524-5

Series: Modern Plays

Typeset by Mark Heslington Ltd, Scarborough, North Yorkshire

To find out more about our authors and books visit
www.bloomsbury.com and sign up for our newsletters.

Nineteen Gardens was first performed at Hampstead Theatre Downstairs, London, on 3 November 2023. The cast was as follows:

AGA	**Olivia Le Andersen**
JOHN	**David Sturzaker**

Writer	Magdalena Miecznicka
Director	Alice Hamilton
Designer	Sarah Beaton
Lighting	Jamie Platt
Sound	Max Pappenheim

Nineteen Gardens

Characters

Aga, *a woman of about thirty to forty, pretty, dressed in an inexpensive but serene way. Perhaps a black top and jeans, trainers. Hair in a ponytail.*

John, *in his fifties, expensive clothes but going for a slightly bohemian look. Corduroy trousers, perhaps a corduroy jacket too. White or blue shirt. Posh. He could be an entrepreneur or a partner at a consultancy.*

The characters in the play often talk in an artificial way, because a lot of what they say is not what they really mean. They are also prone to abrupt, almost unnatural changes of mood.

Act One

Scene One

Aga *is sat at a table in a café, no coffee, and glancing at her phone. She looks businesslike and detached.*

John *appears, looking at his phone, then puts it in his pocket as he comes in. He notices her. Stops. She looks up. Their eyes meet. Music is playing.*

Aga Well hello

John (*coming up to her*) Hello
You look nice

Aga So do you

John No but you

Aga I suppose you didn't expect me
to look anything at all

John What

Aga You probably thought that I wouldn't be in London

John I don't know that I thought anything
(*Smiles.*)
But I know what I'm thinking now

Aga That I would have left the country

John I really didn't

Pause.

But yes I suppose it would have been logical to think
you might have done

Aga The thought must have broken your heart
Knowing how much I wanted to stay
and caring for me like you did

John   Ah
I'm happy that you haven't left though

Aga   Actually
why did you think that I might have done

John   I'm really not sure that I did

Pause.

I mean if I had
it would have been because you are not

Aga   From here

John   Well
Anyone has the right
But perhaps not everybody has got

Aga   The means

John   I suppose not
I mean it's not

Aga   Cheap

John   Well it isn't
Is it
Not for everyone

Aga   So you thought I might have not been able to afford to stay
and left

John   Well
I'm really not sure that I

Aga   It must have distressed you

John   Er
I suppose so
yes
But actually now I'm happy to see that

Aga (*interrupting him*)   Or perhaps
you never thought about it at all

John (*laughing*)   Well yes I was just trying to
A series of relentless tasks at home and at work
My wife my children my houses my meetings my friends my

Aga   Yes
But shall we kiss hello John

John *gets up and stands ready to embrace her.* **Aga** *gets up too. For
a moment, they stand still, close to each other, but don't embrace.*

Music.

Scene Two

The mood changes to tender.

Aga   You smell nice

John   Do I

Aga   Reminds me of wisteria on the facade
of an old country house in Surrey

John (*taking off his coat*)   Why Surrey

Aga   Or another rich place

John *laughs.*

Aga   Where you went for a family getaway
back then

John (*hanging his coat*)
    Why are you saying that

Aga   Just trying to remind myself of what constituted us

John (*sitting down*)   Oh yeah
and what was it

Aga   This thing that
once it starts

then goes on
(*To herself.*) I wonder if it can be stopped

John   What thing

Aga   Inequality

John   You know that's not what it was
We were always equal
Unless perhaps you were my superior
in sensitivity and understanding

Aga   Of the differences in milk prices
between various supermarkets

John (*laughing*)
   Why milk

Aga   Or another cheap thing

John   You know I always thought you superior in many
ways
(*Quietly, glancing around again.*)
to everyone else
And I mean everyone
I never met anyone
who would make a gift of herself
with such generosity

Aga   You mean it was fun hurting me

John   It was fun loving you
and being loved

Pause.

But how are you getting on
It's been a year and a half

Aga   A year and ten months actually

John   Really
How time goes by

Aga   Actually not that fast
When I'm in that hotel of mine

John   Oh yeah
what hotel

Scene Three

The mood changes again. More joking now. They have their drinks.

Aga   Where else would they take a woman of a certain age
and no experience

John   Anywhere should be pleased to take you

Aga   The only experience I had in this country
was in matters of hotels
So there you go

John   I suppose you do have as you say
experience in matters of hotels

Aga   And yes when I'm making beds there
I am sometimes reminded of our good old days

John   Oh I have that too
One thought leads to another
could be age too

Pause.

Not in your case of course
Mine

Pause.

Only yesterday for example I was in Hammersmith
There was a debate at my daughter's lovely school
the same my wife went to
lovely pupils
so very self-assured
when presenting their arguments in support of their thesis
It is only natural that we are entitled to the best things and

others less so
(*Laughing.*)
By the way I wonder what you would say
I bet you would say something

Aga   I doubt it

John   And in the middle of it all
suddenly I was transported
to my uncle's stables
and I saw myself the boy I used to be
coming back from school for the holidays
and running to thank him for yet another term
and then to greet my favourite mare
Her name was Priscilla
She was chestnut
with a little star on her forehead
(*Laughs.*)
Why was I reminded of that
I wonder
perhaps something to do with the way the sun was shining
through the high windows

Aga   Ah really

John   Yes
Funny how our brains work

Aga   Isn't it

Pause.

Last week I found a condom filled with cum
on the pillow
It was tied in a knot so the cum wouldn't trickle out
very thoughtful
It made me think of you

John (*laughing*)   Did it

Aga (*laughing*)   There was a ten pound note underneath
I had no idea what to make of it

John (*laughing*)
   What did you do

Aga   I took it of course
(*With a sudden crazy laugh.*)
The money I mean
not the condom

John   You were always so funny

Aga   Was I
No but you do think it was a tip don't you

John   I don't know
I'm sure it was

Aga   Highlights of that sort don't happen all the time
though
Most days it's just rushing like a crazy person
They always give you less time than you need
managers I mean
Evil people

John (*amused*)   Oh managers always are
aren't they

Aga   Not in your firm I don't think

John   Perhaps not

Aga   Especially that there aren't any managers really
above you I mean

John   Ah yes I suppose not

Aga   And you aren't that evil
to yourself

John   No

Pause.

That's not entirely true
One day I was quite

evil to myself
Very much so

Aga   Ah really

Pause.

And because of the rush you hardly ever actually hoover the
floor
Did you know that

John   No I didn't
(*Laughs.*)
You're more interesting to listen to when you talk about
cleaning
than most people when they talk about Whitehall
Funny that I could have forgotten that

Aga   Did you forget it

John   No not really

Aga   Anyway I couldn't say as I never meet any people who
talk about
Whitehall
Although I suppose I do meet their underpants
Socks too

John   Do you

Aga   The other day there was a pair of really fun socks
Actually one sock
The other one I had to fish from under the bed

John   Oh yeah what kind of socks

Aga   With sort of Lennon's face

John   As in Lennon
John

Aga   Yeah
Or maybe Lenin
Vladimir

John   Right

Aga   Did you know about 50 per cent of people don't flush

John   No I didn't
But that's very funny

Aga   And only about 20 per cent tip
Only Americans really
They do it to make a point I suppose

John   And what point is that
(*Reclines more comfortably in his chair.*)
Tell me

Aga   What's that

John   What point are they trying to make
Americans I mean

Aga   Funny I clean their rooms then maybe they show up
in your office

John   I guess that's possible
So about the Americans

Aga   What

John   Or others
I'm sure you have many good stories
I don't know
Saudi wives shopping for daring underwear
Russians with their perfume bottles full of nerve agents

Aga   There's the woman with a Starbucks cup waiting to
cross the road

John   Oh yes
What about her

Aga (*laughing*)   Being able to afford
something she doesn't absolutely need

John (*laughing*)
    I love the way you speak

Aga   Or the day you realise you shouldn't be buying
washing capsules

John   Buying what

Aga   Washing capsules

John   And why shouldn't you buy washing capsules

Aga   Oh because you can't split them

John   I see

Aga   And suddenly mankind divides itself into
people who buy washing capsules
and people who don't

Pause.

I guess there are also those who don't even know

John (*looking around and bending over the table to be closer to her*)
    How I missed your mind

Aga   But actually the things it is busying itself with
when you run into me let's say in the street

John   Oh I can see now how I have longed for that

Aga   Are not so very interesting
(*Standing up and starting to stroll beside the table as if putting on a
show, making gestures relating to the actions described.*)
Most of the time I am just calculating
do I take the tube and pay 3.30
or do I save 1.80 by taking the bus
but risk being late
The bus is 1.50
What a difference by the way
between bus
1.50
and tube
3.30
1.80
I wonder if the people who set these prices know

how many thousands of daily conundrums
in the field of mathematics
they engender
All these women running late for school pick-ups
because of the 1.80
all this rushing through the streets because of 1.80
and impromptu rehearsals of a variety of feelings
guilt shame resentment not caring the willingness to end it
all

John   Oh no don't say that

Aga   Why not
Am I too obsessed with numbers do you think
A bit like an investment banker
(*Reclining upon the table slightly, while still standing up.*)
The other day
I was walking with my children
they asked
Can we please go to Gail's
our friends all go to Gail's
Children always exaggerate
Do yours too

John (*laughing*)   I suppose so yes
The eldest one said the other day
he thought he played rugby the best of all the boys

Aga   Oh yeah

Pause.

Thea goes to Gail's they say
and Edie goes to Gail's
and Oliver goes to Gail's
they all get cheese straws from Gail's
They're at Gail's all the time
eating cheese straws they say
Children always exaggerate
Do yours too

John   Yes yes

Aga   So I say
I can buy you cheese straws at Lidl
They look at me in despair
They're not cheese *straws* they say
They're cheese *twists*
(*Looking at him intently.*)
You see they know these things

John   Clever children
I'm sure they take after you

Aga   And anyway cheese twists from Lidl are *disgusting* they
say
They have this way of saying *disgusting*
my children
which isn't their own way
which has been picked up at school from other children
So I imagine these other children saying *disgusting*
About all these things that we do
that we have to do
that my children have to
And increasingly so
The number of times they have to do these things
has been increasing
for a year and ten months now
(*Breaks down and cries, but artificially.*)

John   Oh really

Pause.

It is such a good story though
The difference between cheese straws and cheese twists
Gail's and Tesco's

Aga (*rolling her eyes*)   Tesco please

John   What

Aga   Lidl

John   Right

Aga (*sitting down*)   The children are the one thing I can
never forgive myself
That I put them in this situation
That I am teaching them feelings
they ought not know
Useless feelings
Feelings they ought not to have use of

John   Oh my children have strange feelings too
The other day one said he had a premonition
he was going to be prime minister

Aga   This is the thing I will never forgive myself
these lessons in feelings they ought to have no use of
but now they will

John   How I have missed your stories
How I have missed what they remind me of

Aga   And what would that be

John   I don't know
Something that I used to have
and lost

Aga   When did you have it

John   Maybe when I was young
My father taught at university
my mother was into pottery
our house was dilapidated
the family fortune was fading away
apart from the bit that my uncle turned around
and I had no idea yet how it would end
I had no idea that one day I

Aga   Would be so rich and so happy

John   Yes
But there was something I had then

and lost
What was that

Aga   Perhaps
the thrill of the possibility
that one day you might become
so rich and so happy

John (*laughing*)   Yes perhaps

Scene Four

The mood is getting more serious.

Aga   There is the story of a woman who loved a man
She had no idea she would ever love anybody again
On the contrary
she was resigned to a lifetime of sadness
until he came along

John   That's a beautiful story
Love is a beautiful thing
Isn't it

Aga   And bent her life

John (*quietly*)
    How did he bend it

Aga   He took her life like a piece of wire
and bent it
And when he left
her life wasn't a straight thing anymore
but a bent one
funnily shaped

John   Maybe it was a beautiful shape

Aga   Not really I don't think so
He bent her life
and barely noticed

John   And what happened to his life

Aga   Oh nothing
it remained straight as an arrow

John (*looking around and stroking her cheek*)   How I have
missed your mind
and your words

Aga   Do you remember the last ones

John   Last ones

Aga   The last words I wrote
You didn't reply

John   When do you mean

Aga   After that rare day of snow in London

John   Oh yes I was worried you might want to go back to
that
(*Looking her in the eyes.*)
Don't you understand
It was just becoming too intense
Risked destroying things
Encompassing all
Devouring
Turning to ashes
I couldn't risk losing my wife my family to
(*Hesitates.*)

Aga   Especially that we had just learnt my husband had
suspicions
and might take some action

John   Well that wouldn't have been good for me would it
if he found out it was me
It might've
you know

Aga   Bent your life

John   Yes

Aga   But he had found out it was *me*
That was clear wasn't it

John   Well of course
I mean that's what it was
in his message

Aga   And it was all right for my life to be bent
and for yours to continue straight

John   What did you want me to do
I had to think of my children

Aga   And of my children
nobody thought

John   I had a wife

Aga   I had a husband too

John (*laughing*)   Your husband

Pause.

But my wife
And other things of mine
My house my work my friends

Aga   And I

John (*looking her in the eyes*)
   Well

Aga   You mean all I had was a rented flat
and a family that wasn't very happy
and neither was it rich

John   Well that might not sound good but

Aga   We were poor anyway
so it's OK we went to being even poorer
in every sense of the word
While castles like yours
are protected in every storm

John   Your husband already knew
my wife didn't
isn't that true

Aga   Yes

John   You didn't love your husband
I loved my wife

Aga   Oh yes

John   I loved her very much
I still do

Aga   Yes

John   What sense would it have made for me
to go down with you
Would it have made any sense
any sense at all

He looks her in the eyes.

Aga   No

Music.

Scene Five

The mood is sad and tender.

Aga (*quietly*)   That rare day of snow
As we walked across that Chelsea square
you said if I needed anything
anything at all
I should just write to you

John   Did I

Aga   Well and I wrote

John   Yes
I think you might have done

Aga   And I waited for your reply

John   Did you

Aga   Your reply never came

John   I guess it didn't
I guess I was busy
Life just took off
Its relentless stream of obligations

Pause.

You know how it is

Aga   And why did you give yourself the right
to not reply

John   I didn't really
I mean I just

Aga   What gave you the right to not reply

John   Oh I don't know

Aga   You just didn't

John *laughs.*

Aga   Because what

John   I don't know
Because nothing

Aga   Because you could
I suppose

John   Well

Aga   And so the thing I needed your help with

John   What was it

Aga   A thousand pounds
for the lawyer
to find out where to file and how
Before my husband did

and was able to keep whatever money there was
Which is what happened in the end
(*Laughs.*)

John   Was it only that

Aga (*quietly*)   Well

Pause.

maybe

John   And if I had helped you
given you that thousand pounds
it would have changed things

Aga   Perhaps
The law is better here apparently
for a woman in my situation
Sadly she couldn't afford to find that out

John   Well I didn't know that you needed advice

Aga   Because I never had the chance to tell you
because you just didn't respond
You left me completely alone
after all we had
and in a time like that

John   See
(*Looking her in the eyes.*)
That's just what I feared
Maybe that's why I didn't respond

Aga   What a fearful man you are

John (*looking away*)   Yes I feared that you might want me to
be there for you
while I couldn't be there for you
Yes I was worried that you might want to drag me
into the mess of the break-up of your family
while I had to protect my own
Does that sound so strange

Don't you understand
that with all I had
I couldn't take risks

Aga   Yes
And so here I am

Menacing music perhaps.

Act Two

Aga *and* **John** *are in a London street, later. They could stop and sit down on a park bench, etc. every once in a while.*

Scene One

Aga *is walking one step in front of* **John**.

Aga   You know there's one thing that strikes me
when I walk the streets of this city

John   What is it

Aga   It's that people don't draw their curtains
even after dark

John   They don't

Aga   The other day I was walking with my children
It was at the weekend
I wanted to take them to a museum

John   Which one

Aga   In your neighbourhood actually

John   Oh really
What's the name of the museum

Aga   I can't remember

John   You can't remember

Aga   Maybe it wasn't a museum

John   Not a museum

Aga   Maybe it was a church

John   A church
really

Aga   Or a tree

John   A tree

Aga   Or perhaps a house actually
Perhaps I wanted to show them a house
Perhaps I wanted to see it myself

John   A house

Aga   Yes
That might have been it
It started raining
We turned left and right and then left again
and found ourselves in a small residential street
I mean the street was small
The same thing however couldn't be said
about the houses
My children were crying and kicking each other in the rain
They asked can't we just take an Uber home
I said we can't take an Uber home
we'll take a bus
Where's the bus stop they asked
I said we were going to find one
Our feet were getting wet
And there in one of the houses
we saw a woman in a bay window
sat by a small lamp
There was a wall of books behind her
and a poster advertising holidays in the Côte d'Azur
in the 1950s

Pause.

Don't you have one like that too

John   I do

Pause.

Didn't I tell you
I must've done
I don't think you can see it from the street

Aga   Can you not
A small plaque on the window said Remain
and yes one would have wanted to do just that
if one were inside that room like her
A cat lay on the back of the sofa
which was blue
The cat was white
My children stopped and looked
I did too
We were bound by the same dream

John   What dream

Aga   To be there and to own it
or to destroy it

They stop.

Scene Two

John   Well I hope one day you will
I mean own a place

Pause.

I mean why not
You're still young

Aga   Oh I'm sure I will

John   That's the spirit
(*Laughs.*)
One should never lose hope

Aga   I actually gained mine

John   That's wonderful

Aga   It's more than hope
It's certainty

John   All right

Aga   I'm going to buy my own flat soon

John   What kind of flat

Aga   Just a two-bed
I'll sleep in the living room
It's OK
if only I can have my own flat

John   I'm very happy for you
(*He embraces her. Then she pulls away gently.*)
Will you get a mortgage

Aga   Oh no

John   So how

Aga   Oh I have rich friends

They resume the walk. Pause in the conversation.

John   Really
Friends won't buy you a flat

Aga   Won't they

John   People don't just buy each other flats

Aga   Yeah that is rather sad isn't it

John   Someone can buy you a present
like earrings for your birthday
or a book

Pauses.

I could have done that for example

Aga   Yeah that would have been nice

John   Yes
Actually I wanted to back then
then I forgot
Relentless stream of duties
and so on
But this is something that I could've done

Not a flat
I mean your friends won't either
Not a flat
a book maybe

Aga   A book
What about

John   A flat isn't among the things that are done

Aga   Done where

John   Well in
friendships

Aga   Friendships
What about in love affairs

John (*laughing*)   Or even
love affairs

Aga   Really

John   No

Aga   What about in other situations

John   What situations

Aga   Oh I don't know
when would you buy someone a flat
(*Thinking.*)
When you care about them deeply and don't want them to
struggle
for example

John   Well
If I could afford it

Aga   Could you not

John   Me
Could I afford to buy you a two-bedroom flat in London
(*Laughs.*)
Of course I could

Aga   But you wouldn't

John   Well of course not

Aga and **John** *look each other in the eyes.*

Aga   What about in other situations

John   Such as

Aga   For example
what about
blackmail

Scene Three

Change of light, sweet nostalgic music in the background.

Aga   About that story of a woman who had loved a man
the one I started telling you

John   Yes

Aga   What I haven't mentioned yet
is that she had kept his letters

John   Had she

Aga   Lovely letters
Oceans of love poured over her

John   That's a sweet story though

Aga   Waves that bounce you
between soft sands of tenderness
and coral reefs of desire

John   Yes

Aga   That kind of thing
And a lot of it

John   Really

Aga   And with these very minute details of his life

John   What details

Aga   Although he was careful never to mention names in
writing
(*Laughing.*)
So clever
in addition to his extremely beautiful eyes
so blue you could drown in them

John   Oh Aga

Aga   But even he couldn't omit certain details
Neither could she to be fair
Love doesn't like abstraction
It feeds on the down-to-earth
on the precise view from his office window
as he's thinking about her

John   What's the view

Aga   Saint Paul's Cathedral
the south-west tower

John   Surely many have that view

Aga   On the shape of fingernails
widening towards the end like poppy petals

John *glances at his fingernails.*

Aga   On the precise number of back gardens
that separate the lovers' houses

John (*in a hoarse voice*)
   What's the number

Aga   Nineteen
Fancy that
And of course the road and the park
plus the eight floors of my block
But nineteen gardens nevertheless

John   That only narrows it down
right

Aga   Or the date his wife was going to be away
at her UN conference

John (*hoarsely*)   Many people go to these conferences

Aga   And what they can do in that time
With some very graphic descriptions

John   Don't all lovers plan like that
I mean thousands of lovers across the city

Aga   And at which hotel
They might still have the booking details

John   It's doubtful

Aga   Perhaps at another hotel they do
There were many

John   Were there

Aga   Thirty-one to be precise

John (*pale*)   Thirty-one

Aga   Yes
(*Taking out her phone.*)
Would you like me to remind you of some of the names

John   No I wouldn't

Aga   The point is that to an interested party it wouldn't be
hugely difficult
To match a name and a date
with a proof of booking

John   Wouldn't it

Aga   Anyway your wife will surely recognise herself
in the woman with sagging breasts
already at her age
(*To herself.*)
Really why didn't she have something done about them
with all that money

Pause.

I guess why would she
she was loved the way she was

John   I never

Aga   Yes you did
April 21st

John   I must've been crazy
You must've made me crazy

Aga   And thick legs
Well definitely thicker than my
lovely slim legs
(*To herself.*)
Thank God as you say she never wears short skirts
only long dresses from
(*Thinking.*)
Oh I would have to check

John   But I love my wife
and you know it

Aga   I do

John   And I do think she is beautiful

Aga   Yes

John   And I care about her more than about anyone else

Aga   You do

John   And I think it's a privilege for me to be with her

Aga   I'm sure that's true

John   It's just that perhaps she doesn't think the same
about me

Aga   Doesn't she

John   So even if I had written that

Aga   You can discuss this with her

John   I'm surprised by you

Aga   Not positively I understand

John   No

Aga   And I always surprised you positively

John   Yes

Aga   Did I

John   I don't recognise you

Aga   Isn't that a good thing though
the widening of one's horizons

John   How can you do something like this
to someone that you loved

Aga   Don't we only do this kind of thing
to those that we loved
if they hurt us

Music.

Scene Four

John *and* **Aga** *are standing in front of each other under a lamp post. The mood is thick with pain.*

John   I never meant
It was never meant to be something that hurt

Aga   Wasn't it

John   Didn't I tell you from the beginning
this was meant to be good
not bad
It was meant to hold for each of us what we needed most

Aga   Lunches at good restaurants for me

John   Yes
And passion

And for me
passion too

Aga   And the feeling of being
loved unconditionally

John   Well

Aga   That must've been nice

John   It was
Didn't I say though
If at one point you feel that it hurts you more than it pleases
you
we should end it

Aga   What a generous thing to say
to someone in love with you

John   I never meant it to be like that

Aga   You wanted me for my unconditional love
but wished for this love to just stop when conditions changed

John   Maybe I was naive

Aga   Or maybe that was the whole point

John   What

Aga   To have the power to break my heart

She comes up very close to him. Their faces touch, eyes closed.

John   I liked how brittle you were

Aga   How you could make me suffer

John   But I didn't want to
I mean I didn't

Aga   Really care

John   No but

Aga   While with your rich wife
it was only your heart
that could be broken

John   Yes

Aga   It must've been nice
to be able to break someone's
for a change

John (*pulling away*)   Is it my fault that you had nothing to go
back to
that your house wasn't like my house
that your husband wasn't like my wife
that your everything wasn't like my
(*Hesitates.*)
not even everything
like a piece of my something

Pause.

Was it my fault that I was rich and you were poor
and in so many ways
Was it my fault

Aga   No

John   So why punish me for something that I am not
responsible for
For my circumstances

Aga   And all you ever got for your circumstances
was a reward

John   Well

Pause.

Music.

Act Three

In a room. Possibly **Aga***'s small, ugly rented flat.*

Scene One

John *is walking around the room in distress.* **Aga** *is sat at a desk/table, relaxed, and looking at her phone or computer.*

Aga   I'm looking at bedspreads
Oriental blue for my son
Do you know what oriental blue is like

John   I suppose it's oriental

Aga (*laughing*)   Yes
And a bunch of cushions to match
yellow and white and blue
oriental as well

Pause.

For my daughter pistachio green

John   Really

Aga   Does that not sound like the right colour

John   Oh it does I'm sure

Aga   And her cushions will be pink
pink and
(*Thinking.*)
What else do you think will go well
with pistachio green

John   I don't know

Aga   Maybe cream

John   Maybe

Aga   And you know what

Pause.

I have been thinking about it

John   Oh yeah

Aga   And actually
(*Looking up.*)
I've changed my mind
I do want to have my own bedroom too

John   Do you

Aga   Yes
I don't want to sleep in the living room

John   Do you not

Aga   I'm sure you don't sleep in the living room

John   Well
no

Aga (*not looking up from her computer/phone*)   Ah you want to
say you deserve it
Hard work and all

John   Well

Aga   And of whole generations

John   Perhaps

Aga   Mainly of little children in India

John (*rolling his eyes*)   God

Aga   By the way I have started looking
(*Glancing at her phone/computer.*)
No I don't want the impossible

Pause.

I'm not after anything ludicrous
(*Laughing.*)
like the things you have

Like a house in Hampstead
(*To herself.*)
Oh wait
perhaps

John   Aren't you

Aga (*laughing*)   No
There's a three-bed near Alexandra Park
which is a very good school apparently

Pause.

See I'm not asking you to pay school fees
like you do for your children

John   I'm beyond grateful

Aga (*laughing*)   You should be
I could have bid higher
In any case what is it to you
a three-bedroom flat and not even anywhere posh

John   And in exchange for this

Aga   I won't write to your wife

John   You won't

Aga   I will let you keep your life on course
only your bank account will be diminished by some
(*Looking at her phone/computer.*)
750 thousand
I think

John   And if I don't buy you the flat

Aga   Then I won't let you keep your life on course
(*Looking at her phone/computer.*)
I love these wool blankets
They'll be perfect for
(*Mimicking a posh affected accent.*)
curling up on the sofa
during long winter evenings

(*In her normal accent.*)
I'm quoting you

John   Are you

Aga   Yes
That's what you used to write to me
about your family and yourself
(*Mimicking the posh accent.*)
So we have been spending
these long winter evenings
curled up on the sofa
in front of the TV
(*In her own accent, laughing.*)
TV really

John   Did I write that

Aga   Yes
While my family and I
were not curling up on anything at all

John   What were you doing

Aga   I don't know
We were fighting a war

John   Was that my fault

Aga (*not paying him attention*)   But you were so
(*Mimicking his accent.*)
delighted to have met me
which has enabled you to
(*Glancing at her phone/computer and reading.*)
form among the most nuanced and stimulating
experiences of your life
(*Stops mimicking.*)
Meanwhile always being able to go back
to the curling up on the sofa in Hampstead
Which wasn't something I was able to go back to

John   So was that my fault
tell me

Aga   Doesn't mean you can't pay for a flat
where I will be able to curl up
a little bit too
(*To herself.*)
Yes I'll find a nice sofa

Pause.

My God how happy my children will be
As for the blankets
yes the pink one and the blue I think

Pause.

Or perhaps you want to add a housewarming present

John (*standing in front of the window, speaking quietly*)   So this
is what you want
Money
My celestial lover
That's what she's after

Aga   Well yes

John   My sweet woman who never asked for anything

Aga   Yes I suppose this has changed

Pause.

John (*laughing*)   Money
for a three-bedroom flat
really

Aga   And your five-bedroom house
what was it bought with

John   Six-bedroom

Aga   Sorry
What was it bought with
flower petals and snowflakes
the gentle tones of a Bach sonata

John   And it won't be a problem for you
that a sexual relationship will have led you
to fortune

Aga   Let's not exaggerate
just a flat

John   Still

Aga   Your sexual relationship with your wife
didn't it lead you to fortune

John   Well yes
But I had quite enough on my own too

Aga   So it brought her fortune too

John (*laughing*)   Oh she had quite enough not to need
anything at all

Aga   Yes having quite enough
is surely a much worthier thing

John (*looking at her intently*)
    Well

Aga   Nothing compares to having quite enough

Pause.

Now my children will have a bit of that too

Pause.

John *glances at his phone and then puts it in his pocket*

Scene Two

Some minutes later in the same room.

John *walking around the room looking at his phone*

Aga (*still browsing her computer/phone*)   Anything wrong

John   It's Cecilia

Aga   Oh yeah

John   Or rather it isn't her

Aga   Ah
What does she want

John   That's the thing
Nothing
She's not answering

Aga (*looking at her phone/computer*)   Right

John   She doesn't want anything

Aga   Yeah

Pauses.

Speaking slowly, looking at her phone/computer. **John** *is listening to her while looking at his phone.*

My daughter would love to have a cat
Actually my son would love to have a cat too
You know in a rented flat it's pretty much impossible
Landlords never allow anything
Not even a hamster
not even a fish
Unless you grill it
I don't really like cats
But that would make them so happy
That would make them so happy
After all this
do they not deserve a cat

John   Yeah

Pause.

She never wants anything

Aga   What does she not want this time

John   Oh I asked her what she would like for dinner
She said she wasn't coming back for dinner

A work thing
Then I wrote that I missed her
she hasn't replied

Aga   I guess she's got a work thing

John   Yeah

Aga   Oh are you worried it is that sort of work thing
Like the ones you used to have with me

John   No I'm sure not
(*Looking at his phone.*)

Aga   That's good then
I'm reading about cats
Do you know what they say
they say if you are to take a cat
you should take two
(*Laughing.*)
Can you imagine me with two cats

John   Yeah

Aga   Look
she's always been like this
It's just what she is
and you love her

John   Do you think she's out with someone

Aga   Even if she is
what does it matter
She's just like that
and you love her

John   Like what

Aga   Well
I mean closed off from the storms of this world

John   What do you mean

Aga   You know what I mean
just sort of made of stone
She'll make you suffer every once in a while
and she won't even know

John   Why not

Aga   Haven't we been over this before

John   Tell me

Aga   I suppose she somehow doesn't know
what this word means

John   Which word

Aga   You know
Suffer
and other words like that

John   Yes
Why is it so

Aga   She just doesn't do it
She's like a glass that's all full
and doesn't need to be filled anymore

John   Yes

Scene Three

John *comes up to the window and looks out, holding his phone in his hand.*

Aga   Contrary to me

John   What

Aga (*laughing*)   I do seem to always need something

Pause.

back then I needed your love
now I need your money

John   Not only you need things

Aga   Oh yeah

John (*quietly*)   How strange
It's snowing again

Aga (*looking up*)   Is it

Pause.

John (*putting the phone in his pocket*)   And if I say no

Aga   I'll have to push your life off its rails

John   And what if I don't want it on the rails it has been on

Aga   Do you not

John   What if I don't want it the straight arrow that it was

Aga   Why wouldn't you

John   Perhaps I'm tired of it
Perhaps there are other things that I want

Aga   Really

John   Perhaps I don't want the life with my wife
Perhaps I want one with you

Aga   Except that it's not true

John   Perhaps I want all this to change
Perhaps all this time

Aga   One year and ten months

John   One year and ten months
and six days
if you want to know

Aga   Is that right

John   I missed you

Aga   But really you just missed being loved
You would miss not being loved by your wife a million times
more

John   Perhaps I wouldn't

Aga   It's not easy to break a lifelong habit

John   Perhaps I would like to take you on a weekend
getaway

Aga (*laughing*)   God how I dreamed of it back then

John   Perhaps I'll take you

Aga   You never did

John   Perhaps now I will
Would you like that

Aga (*laughing*)   God how I would have liked it then

John   You and me and your kids

Aga   You never let this as much as appear on the horizon

John   Perhaps I will now
Perhaps I don't want to be without you
anymore
Perhaps I don't want
not to be loved
Perhaps I've had enough

Aga   Just give me that money

John   Perhaps you should wait
as a sign of your trust

Aga   But I don't trust you

John (*turning around and looking at her intently*)   And one day
perhaps
you could have much more than a flat

Aga   Will you buy me a whole house or what

John   One day I might want you to share mine

Aga   No you won't

John (*walking around the room, glancing at his phone*)   God she really torments me

Aga   Yes I suppose she always did

John   Won't you hold back for a little while

Aga   Why would I

John   I thought about you
that's the truth
I missed you
this means something

Aga   Well I thought about you too
Every day

Pause.

Wishing you all the evil in the world
Wishing that you should fall under a bus and break your neck
Or at least your heart

John   Did you

Aga   What does that mean
apart from the fact that my heart was broken too

John   I know it was

Pause.

A woman who has a heart
that can be broken
What would it be like
(*Stroking her hair.*)
Aga

Aga   What

John *comes up to her and embraces her.* **Aga** *doesn't pull away.*

Music.

Scene Four

Aga *is lying on a sofa or a bed.* **John** *is walking around the room, sometimes sitting down by her side and stroking her. They speak in a slightly mechanical way which shows they have had conversations like this before.*

John   When I got your email
my heart went out to you

Aga   You must've been bored

John   All of a sudden it dawned on me
how I had missed you
how I had missed what we'd had

Aga   It was a cosy little set-up wasn't it

John   Do you think it's such a common thing
to find somebody who understands
someone you can tell everything
and she'll understand

Pause.

Even about her
you understood

Aga   I did

John   The day I met her
seventeen years ago
in October
Leaves were slippery under our feet
The happiest October I have had

Pause.

Then the October when I met you
and could have both of you
was wonderful too

Aga   Oh right

John   So the October seventeen years ago
such a happy one
followed by a happy November

Aga   Then no less happy December I presume

John   Yes

Pause.

Yes
December too
and so on
Months of bliss and hope when life
which had been crawling for years
suddenly sprang to its feet and sped up
The future was unfolding in front of me
falling into place
a jigsaw puzzle after you have found
the piece you had spent years looking for
Perhaps your whole life up until then

Aga (*laughing, they have found their old camaraderie*)   Surely
not when you were six or seven

John   It was at a dinner party in Primrose Hill

Aga   Isn't that where we went for the first walk
and across Regent's Park and beyond

John   Yes

Aga   Paddington with its wide array of anonymous hotels
may seem far now
Somehow it didn't then

John   She was the goddaughter of a friend of my aunt's

Aga   By the way did you know these hotels
don't feature only in the beginning
and the end
of our affair
but Graham Greene's too

John   She had been abroad

Aga   Yes in Switzerland
where her parents owned
whatever these people own

John   She had only just come back
which was why I had never met her before

Aga   And then you did

John   The moment I saw her
emerging from behind the door
a glass in her hand
and on her face that slightly mocking smile

Aga   Why
Who was she mocking

John   She always has this smile
slightly mocking

Aga   Who is she always mocking

John   I suppose everybody

Aga   Why is she mocking them

John   Oh you've never seen Cecilia

Aga   I never had the honour
no

John (*laughing*)   Yeah it sums it up well
It is an honour to meet her
There's something about her that just makes you feel
flattered
by the mere fact of sharing
the same time and space

Aga   Is there

John   And in that green dress

Aga   What shade

John   Dark
Dark and deep
matching the dazzling green
of her eyes

Pause.

She looked

Aga   What a pity that these things just can't stay that way
That the desire of other things
other people
has to sneak in
and ruin even the most lovely bliss

John   It didn't ruin mine

Aga   Did it not

John   I was always so careful to protect it

Aga   Were you

John   I was careful not to become one of these men
running after the first woman who tickled their fancy
risking the collapse of the things upon which they have built
bigger castles

Aga   Your bigger castle
is still standing

John   It is

Aga   But you did run after somebody

John   Oh I never ran

Aga   Did you not

John   No
I walked
and that never losing my composure
towards a hotel room
where I could indulge in two hours of pleasure

Pause.

and love
And then go back
to the bigger castle

Aga   Yes

John (*stroking her cheek*)   I chose carefully

Aga   Did you

John   If that call of desire you mention happens to all
well for the satiation of mine I chose carefully

Aga   I see

John   Somebody who wouldn't want more

Aga   Of course not

John   Because she wouldn't dare

Aga   How could she
not even being from here

John   Somebody humble
Somebody who felt flattered by the mere interest I showed
her

Aga   Did she

John   Who I knew would step aside the day I said so

Aga   But of course

John (*taking her hand and kissing it*)   The nicest sweetest
woman

Aga   Was I

John   But at the same time quite up to standard

Aga   Well thank you

John   In no way less intelligent
or even of a lesser taste
than the women I meet

Aga   Now you're just being nice

John   Well in matters of the mind
not so much clothes maybe
Some things after all can only be bought with money

Able to give a man all the pleasures
a woman can give
while not holding any powers
because coming from a poor country

Aga (*laughing*)   The advantages of immigration
for the love life of local men

John   I'm sure you never grasped
your own loveliness
How glorious you were in your humility
humble in your glory

Aga   That must've been handy

John   Yes very

Aga   I must've been a dream illicit lover

John   You were

Aga   I suppose they don't come in great numbers
to dinner parties in Primrose Hill
humble women

John (*laughing*)   Not in great numbers no

Aga   Or in any

John   No

Pause.

Do you think it was easy
breaking up

Do you know how many times I woke up missing you
how many dinner parties I sat through

Aga   Were they in Primrose Hill too

John   Or Highgate
or Kew
between the main course and the pudding
suddenly borne back to the taste of your skin
but having to endure chiffon cake with raspberries
and all these lips that weren't yours saying things
that weren't the story of our

Pause.

I imagined what it would be like to be there with you

Pause.

I even started hating my wife
as she lay in bed still as a starfish and as cold
while I galloped through her body hoping to meet yours

Aga (*laughing*)   And did she keep on refusing to give you
head

John   Well
yes

Aga   And she still does

John   Yes

Aga   What a pity

John   I know what you think
You think this means she doesn't love me

Aga (*laughing*)   She clearly considers you revolting
Perhaps she thinks she is doing you a favour as it is

John   Perhaps she does

Aga   But you always loved her that way

John   Perhaps I don't want to anymore

He turns to face the window. **Aga** *comes up to the window too and stands by his side. They're both looking at the snow falling. For a few moments they stand there.*

Aga   Except you will never leave her

John   Perhaps I will

Aga   Just buy me the flat
And do it now

John   How about you give me a little bit of time

Aga   Just give me the money for the flat
and be gone

John   Even with you
in a way it was for her

Aga   How so

John   Wasn't it for her
that I had you
So that my neediness
doesn't put her off

Aga   Yes
I suppose it was

John   Wasn't it for her
that I made two people sad
you and me

Aga   I wonder what it would feel like
to be loved so much

John   My God it felt good
to be loved so much

Aga   Just buy me the flat

John   Listen
just wait for me a little while

Aga   I want my children out of the shit hole we live in

John   I haven't felt so alive in so long

Aga   One year ten months and six days

John   One year ten months six days
(*Looking at his watch.*)
and three hours now
Do you know what it means
to suddenly feel loved

Aga (*quietly*)   Just give me the money

John   No you just give me some time

Aga   For what

John   To find out if I can live without this
If yes I'll buy you your flat
If not you'll be the mistress of my house

Aga   How long

John   Give me a month

Act Four

Scene One

London street. Music.

Aga *is leaving her hotel after her shift and runs into* **John**, *who is walking energetically, beaming with happiness.*

Aga Hi

John Oh hi there
Nice to see you
Is this where you work

Aga Yes

John It's a nice day

Aga Is it

John I have just had a pleasant walk
across the park
had a late and long lunch

Aga Did you

John Do you want to walk a little bit

Aga I have to run
Pick-up time
School
You know if I miss the bus
I'll have to take the tube

John So you'll take the tube

Aga I really shouldn't
You know it's more

She stops.

John What

Aga   Nothing
It's fine
(*She laughs.*)
I keep forgetting
You know I keep forgetting
that everything has changed

John   What has changed

Aga   Well
Or will change very soon

John   Oh really
You mean in your life
that's great news

Aga (*looking at him*)   What do you mean that's great news

John   That things will change for you
Sorry

Pause.

Am I forgetting something you told me
I just had a long and very sweet lunch

Aga   Yes you have mentioned
With whom

John   With Cecilia actually

Aga   Really

John   Yes
We had a nice time
She's really such a character

Aga   Yes
you always said she was

John   Did I

Aga   You did

John   I mean you really can't take her for granted

Aga   No
I suppose you can't be sure to be able to take her at all

John   No
Jesus you're really great
you understand her so well

Aga   I don't really think so
I never met her

John   No
Where would you
I mean yours are two different worlds

Aga   Yes for sure

John   She's incredible

Aga   Yes I recall you saying

John   She's so
so full of things

Aga   That's why she never needs anything

John   That's true
she doesn't

Aga   And you

John   Oh I guess that I just can't stop being charmed by
that

Aga   That's great

John   It really is

Pause. They walk together for a while.

Aga   So I suppose you're not

Pauses.

divorcing

John   Oh no
of course not

And she's gone off that colleague she went out with a few
times
Lucky me

Aga   Yes
(*Quietly.*)
In that case
why don't we just go ahead
with the thing

John   What thing
(*Looking at her intently.*)
Oh you mean

Pause.

meeting

Aga (*laughing*)   No that's not what I meant

John   I would like that though

Aga   I thought you were back in love with your wife

John   I was never out of love with my wife

Aga   I guess not
Well let's just go ahead then

John   All right
What about Paddington
And its wide array of anonymous hotels
I should be able to find one
What about Wednesday week

Aga (*stopping and facing him*)   What about your wife
You're not afraid she will find out
about this time

Pauses.

There are also the times before

John   Oh she won't mind

Pause.

Aga (*pale*)   She won't mind you making love to me

John   No
God she's a character isn't she
Actually she doesn't really care
I have found that out
I should have always known it

Aga   Right
Anyway that's not what I meant
I meant let's go ahead

Pause.

with the flat

John   What flat

Aga   The one for me and my children

John (*laughing*)   Oh
Sorry I have so many things going on
relentless series of duties at home and at work
dinner party after dinner party
one even tonight
in Primrose Hill actually

Pause.

Yes maybe at that party
I will be thinking of you again
Of seeing you soon
May I do that

Aga   What

John   May I let my mind drift away
from the absolutely thrilling things
all these marvellous friends of ours
most of them in law and finance
have to say
while they dig into their

leek carpaccio
and fantasise about

Aga   Sure

John   Your lovely body and your wild mind
May I

Aga   Of course
I have been looking

John   And anyway I'm sure Cecilia will soon find
another colleague she'll like
On the first trip probably
She's going on one in two weeks' time
I'll need some moral support

Aga   I have been looking
The one I showed you in Bounds Green is fine
but actually there's a slightly nicer one a few streets down

Pause.

It doesn't matter
the one I showed you would be great
We're lucky it went down
Remember it was 750
It's 725 now

John   Oh
that
your little blackmail thing

Aga   Yes

John (*laughing*)   I would've forgotten

Aga   Would you

John   I told her everything ages ago

Aga   You told who

John   Well Cecilia
who else

Aga   Ages

John   Well a few days after you and I met
It was nice of you to have given me that time

Pause.

Real act of trust

Aga   What did you tell her

John   Oh I told her the whole thing
About you and me and how you wanted to blackmail me
or else you would
(*Quotes her, pompously, laughing.*)
bend my life like I have bent yours
push it off its tracks as yours had been pushed

Aga (*quietly*)   You did

John   Yes

Aga   And what did she say

John   Oh she was vaguely amused
Then she talked about that conference she's going to
In Geneva
She thinks it is going to be fab

Aga   And the letters

John   Ah yes
I even wanted to read her some passages
you know so she wouldn't be shocked or something
in case you really did send them

Aga   And

John (*laughing*)   The thing is
she wasn't that interested

Aga   She wasn't

John   She's a real character
She's so

She's so full of
You know when you said she didn't need anything
she even doesn't need
a particularly faithful husband

Laughs.

Aga   Oh
doesn't she

John   No
God was I lucky
to marry her

Aga   Looks like you were

John   God yes

Pause.

Aga *(quietly)*   So about my flat

John   What about it

Aga *(quietly)*   Will you still
buy it

John   A flat for you

Aga   Yes

John   It's a strange thing to ask a man
to buy you something that costs what
750 thousand pounds

Aga *(eagerly)*   725 now
You know if that's too much
We can go for two bedrooms
I can sleep in the living room
a two-bedroom would be 550 maybe
Perhaps 500 even
something like that

John   I mean it takes me a couple months to make
that kind of money

And my investments
I mean ours
Cecilia's and mine
don't grow by that sum in a day either
and what if the stock market goes down

Aga (*quietly*)   Otherwise I will never be able to buy one

John   No I don't see how you will

Aga   So

John   So what

Aga   If not out of fear
couldn't you buy it out of
something else

John   Like what

Aga   I don't know

John   What a thought
(*Laughs.*)
What would I tell Cecilia

Aga (*quietly*)   I don't know
Maybe she wouldn't find out

John   But what if she did

Aga   Maybe she wouldn't care
like she doesn't about other things

John   But what if she did care
How can I know

Aga   You could risk it

John (*laughing*)   I can't risk her anger

Aga   But you did just risk it
telling her about us

John   Yes but this was a different kind of risk

Aga   Was it

John   I had to do it for her
For my relationship with her
Your blackmail thing would have been a looming shadow
But there's no need to take that risk now

Aga (*quietly*)   Not for her no

John   Well
you see

Aga   Yes

John   Doesn't this make things easier though

Aga   I don't know does it

John   Isn't this a nicer thing
a world where some people can
but not others
Some can
others can't
and there's nothing that will change this

Aga   I guess so

Starts walking away into the snow.

John (*running after her, shouting*)   You can't
but I can
Isn't this a simpler world

Aga   Yes

John   Oh just stop and kiss me
Undo your coat
I want to feel your body

Aga   I'll miss the bus

John   Take the tube

Aga   I can't

John   Oh fuck it just take the tube
and kiss me
Let's just go back to what we had
Weren't we happy
Wasn't that good
I want a little bit of you
I want a little bit of this

Aga   Sorry I can't
I'll miss the bus

John   Oh God stay
I don't know how I will do without you
I really don't know how I will do without it

Aga *disappears and* **John** *stands there, murmuring, then sits down in the snow. Music. Light going down.*

Then lights go up, and we hear the clamour of conversations, clinking of glasses, like at a party, although we can't see it. **John** *gets up, shakes the snow off his trousers, starts walking, first slowly, then energetically in the opposite direction to* **Aga***'s.*

The end.

Printed in the USA
CPSIA information can be obtained
at www.ICGtesting.com
LVHW020937171024
794056LV00003B/814

9 781350 455221